GOD AND GOSPEL

A Dual Perspective

Think you know it
Think again

Michael J Spyker

AgapeDeum

Published in Adelaide, Australia by AgapeDeum
Contact: agapedeum.com

ISBN Paperback   978-1-7637149-2-2

    Ebook   978-1-7637149-3-9

Copyright © Michael J Spyker 2024
All right reserved. Other than for the purpose and subject to the conditions prescribed under the *Copyright Act*, no part of this publication may be reproduced, stored in a retrieval system, or transmitted in any form or by any means, electronic, mechanical, photocopying, recording and otherwise, without prior permission of the publisher.

Publication assistance by Immortalise

Cover design: Ben Morton

Cover photo by Michele Ferrari

Oh, Gospel fire, cool and calm
A steady burn that does no harm
The heart aglow in high or low
His presence felt so deeply

CONTENT

Chapter 1	A Good News Journey	1
Chapter 2	A Divine Perspective	4
Chapter 3	A Human Perspective	7
Chapter 4	Believing	10
Chapter 5	Free Will	13
Chapter 6	Power of Love	16
Chapter 7	Visions	19
Chapter 8	Sin	22
Chapter 9	Creation	25
Chapter 10	The Trinity	28
Chapter 11	Redemption	31
Chapter 12	Resurrection	34
Chapter 13	A New Creation	37
Chapter 14	I AM	40
Chapter 15	A New Spirit	43
Chapter 16	Come	46
Chapter 17	Religion	49
Chapter 18	The Preacher	52
Chapter 19	With the Flow	55
Chapter 20	In this world, not of it	58
Chapter 21	Best Wishes	61

1
A Good News Journey

When in my twenties I became enthused with God's Good News and the excitement has never left me since. 'Think you know it, think again' became the guiding principle of my understanding with many benefits both spiritually and practically. My many questions of what personhood really was about were answered with spiritual theology and mystical tradition being particularly helpful. I have been reading in religion, philosophy as well, and psychology. Today, I am more convinced than ever of the central importance of the Gospel to our world. In every sense that wisdom is primary. The Lord's Good News is ever relevant. It is kind, full of love and uniquely personal. It enhances personhood and creativity.

In my search for truth I understood that for the Gospel to be effective in living it out, it best be rather simple. It is the only way in making success possible. Such simplicity would allow for a concentrated focus on what

I would aim to be about. Keep it simple – keep it focused. Though simple, it needed to be a profound way of life and meet the requirements beneficial to psycho-spiritual wellbeing. Moreover, it should extend mere knowledge and connect with the transcendent. I have always considered myself to be a person with spiritual tendencies. Needless to say, God's Good News meets all these requirements and is relational in a unique way. It not merely informs, but helps towards proficiency in what it encourages.

My involvement with the Lord has taken its time in developing. Figuring out the essential and what to focus on revealed itself progressively. It took a while in coming to appreciate the Gospel's full magnificence as nobody really ever told it succinctly from beginning to end; not to me anyway. The full story is needed for its significance to become properly understood. Next, you have to figure out what it might mean at a deeper level. Much reflective prayer and becoming acquainted with the history of Christian spirituality have been a help. I will use these insights in explaining what the Gospel means to me. Whatever idea you may come across while reading on that seems a bit different, it is not new but based on those who have come before.

A major question regarding our existence is how an all-powerful God of love can allow a world so full of pain and suffering. Love, as the power of all that is good, is so totally opposite to sin – the destruction, pain and death we are exposed to. Love and sin are both operative in our world. It may be expected that the Gospel would address this situation and in a manner that will satisfy the believer. However much, to a large extent, mystery remains in play.

Much depends on how the Good News is explained. I suggest a two-pronged approach. God's plan for creation must be told taking a divine perspective and also a human one; while the difficulties in reconciling the two must be considered. Moreover, what is needed at a personal level, both spiritually and psychologically, in best internalising the benefits on offer when taking the Gospel to heart, also needs discussing.

2

A Divine Perspective

Scripture tells us that creation was spoken into being by God out of nothing. God acted, in accordance with the divine nature, and it was there. God, as ultimate being, could not create but in accordance with that nature, which is summed up in three words: God is Love. Creation is an act of divine love. A simple statement, but of enormous significance.

The mystics and seers of all major religions have perceived that what exists essentially issues from a power we call love. Such an observation can be made because as people we are able to recognise what love is about. But we have no idea of the power and magnitude of a love that is divine. It is beyond our imagination. Love, to us, is a feeling. Not so to God. God *is* Love. The very being of God is love. God cannot but love, always. In doing otherwise, if that were possible, God would deny the divine nature.

When God created it was intended to be perfect and everlasting; an intent that hasn't changed. The divine plan for creation still is one of beauty and joy with its final manifestation yet to eventuate in what is called Heaven. Presently, the picture to us is quite different. The world is in deep strife and always has been. Suffering and death abound. Considering our world an expression of love seems fanciful. Still, great good is done by humanity while exposed to evil. Everything good reflects the nature of God from whom life and the good originates. God is ever active, though that is mostly hidden.

That creation exists as an act of love is a mystery to us. Important aspects of this mystery have however been revealed. None more so than God's divine plan for our world and its unfolding from beginning to end. In broad brushstrokes it may be known – a mixture of revealed facts and divine intent.

The broad brushstrokes that depict God's plan paint a simple picture. The Gospel is not difficult to understand. Anyone so inclined will find the story quite easy to access. It is a reasonable story that holds together well, to a point. A willingness to believe in facts that are beyond reason and must be accepted as true simply because God reveals them as such, is needed.

Understanding the Gospel has two levels that invariably will confront us. One level invites us into considering the unfolding of creation from God's perspective with divine love as its focus. It is the superior way of gaining insight. But unavoidably, as people living in an imperfect world with all its troubles, we cannot but bring the Gospel down to earth, so to speak, as well. It is the other level. Besides being divine, God's Good News is also a human story – very much so.

3

A Human Perspective

A valid and often asked question is: 'Why, if God is good and all powerful, are we living in such a suffering world?' The honest answer to this is that presently we are living a halfway existence. The end, as yet, is not in sight, but it will be magnificent. Not much help right now, you might say and I would agree – mostly. For now, it is what it is, and much of it is not of our doing. But, much of it is. The problem started right from the moment God began to create and it is called sin.

When God created as an act of love, it seems that the power of sin got an immediate foothold. The reason for it we will never know. Right from the start of creation a power of disintegration became operative which shows in that everything will die and often by being killed by another. The animal world survives in doing so while frequently people seem to have no qualms killing each other either. Sickness and death, everything that makes suffer, happens because of sin being inherent in creation. All that brings life, health and what is good, expresses the power of love.

It is not our fault that we are 'sinners' and we will not be held accountable for that by God, unless our sinful inclinations become morally evil. Evil is a choice of truly bad behaviour that can be avoided and thus is open to divine evaluation.

The limitations placed upon us by living in a world of good and evil make being clear-sighted on what God is like difficult. The history of humanity is one of seeking to pierce what is clouding spiritual realities. It has resulted in many systems of belief. This search is not wrong in itself, but it can result in legitimising destructive practices. How many warring efforts have not taken place, and are, in the name of 'god'? How much questionable authority being brought to bear upon believers? Christianity does not escape this reality. The God we like best may be one largely of our own making. Understanding God correctly can easily escape a person.

That applies to all people. Everyone is confronted with a God 'hidden', due to the nature of personhood. We are all looking into spiritual darkness to a large extent. For that reason Jesus declared himself to be the 'Light of

Life.' He came to explain what God 'really' is like; something the people of his day had not been taught and even today is insufficiently understood. Jesus came not merely to talk about the love of God but, more so, to solve the problem of sin. It is what the Gospel is about.

A human perspective on God will always be imperfect. A particular drawback presents when divine realities are made overly subject to the power of reason. Our limited understanding of God may be overcome by considering God's perspective on our plight; by taking a divine view on what life is about. For that to be properly effective the power of 'believing' is key.

4

Believing

Beauty is in the eye of the beholder, so they say. One person's beauty needs not be another's. The eye is guided by what someone 'believes' to be beautiful. So much in life is shaped by a uniquely human ability – by that of believing.

My outlook on life derives much from the rational ideas I hold. Still, what are some of those ideas based on? I am not a machine, though modern materialists seek to convince me simply to be a bio-chemical manifestation. I have feelings though and materialists cannot determine why this is so. Somehow, I feel extended beyond myself, sensing the presence of a greater reality. My approach to this depends on societal influences and personal belief.

Believing is a powerful human dynamic. I may wonder about God. The capacity of reason alone is not able to definitively prove God's existence. Many clever people have tried and ultimately failed. The way towards God is the way of believing. There is nothing fanciful about it. Most of humanity has believed in a spirit world one way or another. The modern conviction that 'God is dead' deep down is based on belief also.

Being so common, the influences of believing are too easily taken for granted. In history much progress has been made by people following through on what they intuitively felt to believe in. The sciences are but one example of that, when ideas becomes verifiable. Every person goes through life believing, whether right, wrong or indifferent. What I believe about myself, is who I consider myself to be. Whole worldviews are constructed on what is believed to be true or false.

The idea of God also is subject to belief. Such as, which aspects of the divine revelation am I willing to accept? I am confronted with mysteries and facts. It is a mystery that Jesus is the Son of God and a fact that he walked the earth. It is a mystery that God created our universe out of nothing, but a fact that I am living in it. Many of God's mysteries are open to interpretation. An important point however is, that mysteries involving the Gospel are not. They are to be accepted as fact, without fail. If not, the Gospel story, and its power, loses its coherence.

This divine story presents us with a take it or leave it

invitation. Bringing a human perspective to it, marred by the inevitable influences of sin and seeing in a mirror dimly, is unhelpful. The Good News originates from a higher level of existence than ours and must be accepted as such.

The way to God is the way of believing in divinely revealed facts. That God is love and Jesus is the Son. That Christ has completely disempowered sin once for all with magnificent eternal consequences. Insights that have come to light through the Lord himself and by spiritually gifted believers of the past. Of course, the Gospel must make cohesive sense as well and it does. I believe in it.

5

Free Will

Beliefs arrive, are modified and may fade away. Their permanency is a matter of choice and dedication; a factor that features heavily in the Gospel. The future of creation depended on the choices made by Christ while he walked the earth. Wrong ones, and the power of sin ingrained in creation would not be defeated. Right ones, and Jesus had a chance of victory. It was up to him.

We are aware of having a will. It determines personhood, which has fascinated many thinkers throughout history. Spinoza considered a person's life scripted in every detail by God and thus making free will irrelevant. Immanuel Kant held that free will is the same as being morally responsible, while Nietzsche suggested that a true sense of freedom derives from a person's innate will to power that must be embraced and cultivated. He considered the idea of having a free will scathingly. Many theologians and philosophers have considered the meaning of free will.

That will may be restricted due to circumstances but even so it will manifest in some way.

Willing freely involves making choices in accordance with preferences. Good ones, inconsequential choices and also bad ones. The importance of it is shown in the creation story involving Adam and Eve: should they eat of the forbidden fruit or not? It foreshadowed the test Jesus was to face on the cross in sticking to the excruciating choice of doing what his Father desired. The universe's salvation was at stake. The successful outcome of God's plan for creation pivoted on the human capacity of free will. That of Jesus, the Son of man – God as a person.

Whatever I believe in, it will be open to doubt. The very nature of believing makes it so. A measure of uncertainty is always present whether acknowledged or not. I am free to doubt as much as to believe and can respond as I see fit. Firmness of belief depends on how much I will stick to what I hold to be true. Always, my beliefs will be challenged by lingering doubt for such is human nature. I may believe in the Good News, but will my faith stand the test of time?

The answer to that question involves mental consistency

in what I have concluded as being true – with affirming feelings towards the positive. I must engage with the mysteries of God not just willingly, but *wilfully*. Set my mind to accepting Gospel facts as indisputable. Not like the glorification of human willpower ala Nietzsche, but with a dependency on God's Spirit. Ask for it and an enablement of grace towards believing will be given. So naturally, that it easily escapes detection unless accepted by faith. Grace firms up the soul.

    In much of life exertions of the will come naturally. Not so in matters that clearly demand choices. When significant, they must be carefully considered and the will becomes activated accordingly. The more important the choice, the more it must be wilfully attended to. Without wilfulness nothing of substance will ever be achieved whatever the situation. Likewise, only wilfulness will ever release the Gospel's full effects. It's time to have a closer look at this Good News story.

6

Power of Love

Love makes the world go 'round, more so than many realise. That mystics and seers of major religions understood love to be the foundation of all that is created has been mentioned. Love is the power that defines what God is like. Apostle John declared that God *is* Love. Whosoever does not know love, does not know God, he taught. In getting to know God, taking love seriously is a must. Without throwing some love about my Christianity becomes questionable.

If that seems quite a task then what expresses love is not well understood. Love must not be seen as mostly a feeling, all warm and affectionate. Any act of goodness, God will see it as an act of love. Any well-meaning intent likewise. Perhaps a better word to use is charity. As such, our loving is more active than we might have thought.

A comprehensive approach to the meaning and nature of love will include both a divine and human perspective.

The two are related, but should not be confused. God's reality of love is very much higher than ours. The two are hardly comparable but for the fact that I, as a person, have an idea what love is like. That idea needs multiplying to the extreme in considering the love of God.

God doesn't see me like I might imagine. Marred by sin I will not ever be fully positive regarding my state of being. When engaging with the Lord the idea that I am not that loveable will raise its head. It is true enough, but carries no weight before the deep love of God. God *is* Love and loves unconditionally anyone, lock stock and barrel. We are all divinely loved and doubtful human perspectives on it change nothing.

Accepting this wholeheartedly will not come naturally. We are conditioned to consider God as a bit scary, to say the least. Like Adam and Eve, who once having eaten from the forbidden fruit began to hide. It is a normal reaction due to the inescapable influences of sin within the human soul. God understands the problem and Jesus came to undo it by defeating sin on the cross. Not just partially, but altogether – sin's every expression throughout all of creation. From the furthest galaxies to the innermost of the earth. That is Good News.

It may be concluded that any perceived barrier between God and people is a mere illusion. Not accepting this as true does a disservice to what Christ has achieved and will limit Gospel understanding. Predominantly, the Church and its history have portrayed God by taking a human perspective, that of sinner's guilt. Unless counterbalanced with the divine view of people's plight, that all are deeply loved and unreservedly so, the meaning of the Gospel becomes lopsided.

7
Visions

Insights into divine reality often occur by believers having a vision. As God is Spirit, it should be no surprise that spiritual engagements bring understanding. The idea that, 'God *is* Love', is supported again and again by mystical experience. Once, fairly early in my ministry, it happen to me. The Lord briefly lifted the veil a little that shrouds the reality of divine love. I cannot describe what it was really like, but ever since, this vision has underpinned my approach to spiritual theology and personhood. It was clear to me that none is more important than understanding the love of God.

In my view, nobody has expounded this better than Lady Julian of Norwich (1342-c. 1423). Once sick unto death in bed she had 16 visions of Christ on the cross; the deep suffering and the victorious outcome. She spent decades after praying and interpreting what she saw in the solitude of being an anchoress. Her insights are incredible, but acceptable in light of the depth of divine love having no end. The Lord showed that if he would have had to suffer for every person individually, he would gladly have done so. Just imagine?

Julian was particularly enamoured by how kind and familiar the Lord is. How appreciative of anyone doing their best in getting life right, particularly those who involve him. He is always near and a very present help in trouble. Her visions were representative of what life on earth is like and included the vexing question of suffering. It may be said that her account straddles the complexity of divine and human perspectives on creation well. She called it a higher and lower contemplation.

At times, her questions found not much of an answer. When asking the Lord about sin, the response simply was: 'sin is necessary'. She felt it best not to enquire further. When addressing suffering the answer mostly was that it is unfortunate, but the Lord is close and a helper. Once in Heaven all will be explained to our satisfaction. She would have to accept that. The great love she saw made these divine statements palatable, knowing that creation is in a process towards perfection.

A major point was that the teachings of Holy Church didn't always align with what her revelations taught her.

This was particularly so with regard to sinners being lost to God. Jesus acknowledged the issue but said that what people cannot fathom, is possible with God. Julian's most famous statement that often appears in her writing is that: 'All will be well.' One day God will do a great deed and make all things well.

Julian's Revelations are readily available these days. My novel *Julian's Windows* contextualises them in a modern love story. The reason for this chapter is to accentuate the problem of a higher and lower perspective of the Good News. Both are valid, but when they don't correlate the higher one must have prominence. God is relational and not religious.

8
Sin

The existence of sin is a horrible mystery. Sin has no substance and is sin because it is not God, Lady Julian concluded. Where God offers love and what is good, sin involves disintegration and evil. With the power of life originating with God, that of death belongs to sin. Why sin exists at all we shall never know. That its influences run far deeper than morally wrong behaviour is a given. It may be assumed that sin has been operative from the very beginning of creation. Long before people walked the earth suffering and death abounded. I believe, that in creating God was faced with the fact that sin would infiltrate and needed dealing with over time. As creation exists in Christ, the Son of God, it would be he who was to undo that ugly spiritual power called sin, forever. This happened on a cross at Calvary. It is Good News.

The reason for sin having legitimacy will ever remain hidden behind an impenetrable cloud of divine wisdom.

At least the Gospel, unlike other religions, recognises sin for what it is and declares the problem solved. What sin is about altogether was not soon recognised. In the three synoptic Gospels the word sin hardly appears. It became prominent in Apostle Paul's theology, and in the Gospel of John thereafter. John considered sin to be a matter of morality and ethics – that of not loving your neighbour and twisting the truth about Christ.

Love and sin are the two primary spiritual influences within creation. As people we are subject to both. All that is good reflects the nature of God. All that is bad reflects sin. God brings life, while sin destroys it. There are small acts of love and large ones. There are minor acts of sin and evil ones. The ability to love is not exclusive to people and is to be found in the animal world as well. Care and courting are not uniquely human. The animal world is burdened under the power of sin with sufferings and killing. But it knows not evil. That moral choice belongs with humanity. Minor mistakes made by us are part of life and God understands. When engaging purposefully in destructive immorality the realm of evil is entered. Such behaviour will be scrutinised by the Lord.

It may be thought that God being perfect and at rest is

impervious to suffering. Nothing could be further from the truth. The suffering of Christ on the cross translated into the Trinity without reduction. The suffering of our world is a suffering within a Love of God that will never disassociate itself from any aspect of creation. It is what divine love is about. I am not even trying to get my head around this. It is too marvellous for me.

Sin found its expression as soon as God created. The creation happened anyway. The only acceptable reason to present is that the final outcome of the creation process would be more than worth it to God, and to our world. Apostle Paul writes: 'I consider that the sufferings of this present age are not worth comparing with the glory that is to be revealed to us' (Rom. 8:18). He includes the whole of creation in this statement.

9

Creation

Scripture paints the picture of there being nothing, God spoke, and creation came into being. Science proposes that our universe came to be through a 'Big Bang' that over eons of time developed in what we are confronted with today. That our universe is very old science can readily prove, but not so the Big Bang. Nor how out of a myriad of interacting atoms eventually life came forth in its countless manifestations. I believe that our universe is the expression of intelligent design: God's handiwork. This creative act keeps on developing throughout the ages. From a divine perspective the life of our universe is readily overseen, God being beyond space and time and all-knowing. A human perspective is faced with accepting the origin of creation's existence, and its continuation, by faith in accordance with revelation.

Every aspect of creation is indwelled by the love of God. Christian spirituality teaches that deep within every soul there is an active presence of this love. Not that anyone would notice. Very seldom does that presence reveal itself and if so only briefly to those steeped in contemplation. In my book *The Primacy of Love* I have discussed the idea of eternal and universal love. Eternal love is the essence of God, while creation exists in universal love. Universal love is a derivative of eternal love. But never will the two disconnect for the nature of God's Love makes that impossible. However much universal love is marred by sin, eternal love will not disown it.

Creation functions in accordance with divinely set laws. God has deemed it fit for people to be able to investigate those. Science and technology are a testimony to it. As are insights into the human psyche and also matters of a spiritual nature. Altogether it makes a wonderful tapestry of knowledge. Quantum physics acknowledges that at its most primary, all is energy. Love nor sin have substance. They surely are dynamic and as such an energy. It may be thought that essentially creation consists of spirit. I have discussed this in my book *Science and Spirit*.

These kinds of deduction are philosophical theology. Paul Tillich held that frequently theology is philosophical and I concur. God is Love. God is Spirit. That creation would derive from these two realities, makes sense. It then also makes sense that changing the nature of the spirit in which creation exist, the dynamic of that love/sin, will change creation. Pull sin out and a suffering world will become one exclusively enveloped by love. Universal love will have been 'reborn'. Heaven arrives.

This has been achieved by Christ. It is what the Gospel is about. Not as an interesting story, the heralding in of a new beginning for all that is. The total uprooting of sin has been accomplished. The Trinity knows that victory to have been won. From a human point of view, as yet, it doesn't seem that way one bit. The power of sin remains discouragingly active.

10

The Trinity

The idea of God presents to us as three divine Persons: Father, Son and Holy Spirit. They are without gender. Motherhood is likewise ascribed to God, who birthed creation in the Son. This Trinity is holy and perfect, and without any secrets between them. They are One God, undivided, but with each Person having a particular function. The Father created in the Son by the power of the Holy Spirit. As a divine unity they are impervious to sin. The Trinity is Love and at rest.

However, divine love seeks to share and reach out as much as possible spreading itself far and wide. It meant creating a reality that derives from the Trinity, but would not be divine. Divine reality is complete and perfect. By introducing a created reality, that is extending from the divine but is not itself so, the problem of sin arose. Sin was waiting to pounce and infiltrate God's creation. The three Persons were aware of this.

Sin is a mystery in that while its destructive powers are known, its origin is not. It is an ever threat to all that is and is not divine. A threat at the most primary level of creation. Safeguarding God's creation against sin could not simply happen by divine command. The power of sin has legitimacy. It needed defeating at its own level of being, that of belonging to God's creation. Only love, so completely other, would be able to accomplish this defeat. The confrontation between love and sin was to take its time however and, for reasons only God knows, creation would suffer.

The power of love was to eradicate sin from creation once and forever. But in doing so sin would be given an opportunity to show itself the more powerful and remain. The challenge to its legitimacy could backfire on love. At least, it could from sin's perspective. The fight needed a level playing field at which both love and sin are operative – that of creation.

The Father, by the power of the Holy Spirit, created in the Son, in whom everything exists. The Son is the Word, Apostle John wrote, the personification of divine creative expression. And the Son was to take responsibility for a suffering creation that holds together in him. The Word became flesh, John explained, and lived among us. The

Son was born a human being.

The divine plan was that in defeating sin through love, the Son fulfilled his destiny. The creation existing in him would enter a new beginning, free of sin's ravishes and death and thus everlasting. Reborn, creation would come to exist both in the Son as a divine being and in the Son as a new creation human person. Everyone would follow him in one day into Heaven in the same renewed likeness, though not divine.

This is the creation story explained from a divine perspective. It may not seem of much help to our present situation in a deeply troubled world. God identifies with suffering and decided it to be unavoidable – for now. It would be deep, divine suffering that was to open up creation's designated eternal future. God paying the ultimate price for it to become possible.

11

Redemption

A human take on the idea of God has a mixed history of fine prophecy and beautiful poetry, and instances in the name of God that in no way correspond with the divine nature of love. Sin makes it inevitable. What God is like becomes adapted to culture and leadership preferences. Religion, as a portal to God, can become and end in itself focusing on ritual, dogma and tradition. The idea of God became revealed to Israel over time and has often been misunderstood. A high point of this revelation occurred with the arrival of Jesus of Nazareth. He was at pains to explain God's immediate presence and love, but religious authority branded him a heretic to die on a cross.

Jesus, walking the streets and the dust of Israel, had not expected otherwise. His miracles, stories and instructions sought to explain a loving God and ways of living wisely. As he would have expected, it was to no avail. He never expected to change the religious authorities, for it was not possible. Rather, his mission was to eradicate the reason for their stubbornness being a spiritual blindness due to the dynamics of sin active in their souls. It is a problem facing everyone.

Jesus carried his cross, and the burden in his soul of his Father being so misunderstood, painfully unto the hill of Calvary. The greatest event in the history of creation was unfolding. Universal love and sin were to face off, with only one to achieve ultimate authority. The destiny of God's handiwork was at stake. Only Jesus knew the real reason for his coming to this desolate place of suffering. To redeem a lost creation that is meant to be perfect.

People have been created in the image of God. In many ways they are like God, but for sin. This image enabled the Son of God to humble himself and become human without thereby losing the essentials of the divine nature. Jesus was born a baby in Bethlehem. He lived under the power of sin bodily, but in his spirit never sinned. In human terms it would mean that he was morally perfect. Apostle Paul could later declare him to have known not sin.

Moral behaviour is a choice and Jesus was sticking to doing right in submitting to his Heavenly Father's wish of not giving up on defeating sin. It brought victory at a heavy price. Only within people do good and evil coexist. Only in a person would a confrontation between those two forces be possible. God had designed it so from the beginning, thus exposing sin's Achilles heel.

Under immense suffering, Jesus the Saviour, the one who was without sin, was facing off with Satan, the ultimate personification of evil. We can't imagine what this battle involved. It was an all or nothing conflict Whatever Satan threw at Jesus was absorbed within his personhood out of love for his Father and the creation. Apostle Paul understood that in the process Jesus himself actually became sin. Love emptied out the power of sin and evil completely, once and forever. Those standing at the foot of the cross had no idea what was taking place. With his last breath they heard the Lord say: 'It is finished'

12

Resurrection

From God's perspective the battle had been won. To the disciples it seemed that years of following Jesus had been in vain. Jesus body was laid to rest in a cave with a large stone rolled before its opening. The day after his death being the Sabbath, it was on the third day (our Sunday) that two disciples, both named Mary, ventured to pay their respects at the tomb. Stunned, they discovered that the heavy stone had been rolled away and Jesus' body had disappeared. An angel came to tell them not to be afraid, Jesus had risen! The celebration of that day came to be known as Easter Sunday.

Years later, Apostle Paul would explain that unless the resurrection of Jesus is accepted as fact, there is no point in becoming a Christian. Paul never witnessed the event but Apostle John did, who humbly refers to himself as 'the other disciple' in his telling (John 20). He recounts much of what had happened that first Easter. How that evening Jesus appeared to them all. Being afraid of Jewish authorities the disciples were huddled together in a room firmly shut off. Jesus entered through a wall as if from nowhere and wished them 'Peace'.

Jesus would have said 'Shalom'. It encapsulates total wellbeing for people individually and societies. It involves compassion and kindness, not just to people known but to strangers as well. Communities living together with nothing to make them afraid because God would be with them. It reminds of Heaven, the eternal Shalom.

The promises of God to Israel were founded on the principle that if you behave well, I will look after you. Based on reading God's covenants in the original Hebrew, contemporary Jewish scholar Dr Naomi Wolf comments that in practising mercy and care the Israelites become God's people. It is shalom principles that bring wellbeing and security to a people. God's promises are conditional.

Firstly, God's covenants are relational. The divine nature is not religious or nationalistic. Shalom is for everyone and its promises are for all to make happen, believer and non-believer alike. In shalom human love finds its most rounded expression. Its potential indwells every person. God cares for shalom people irrespective of race and culture. God will nurture their personal shalom.

After wishing them peace, Jesus blew on his disciples saying 'receive holy spirit.' He had foretold this to happen when meeting Nicodemus, as is recorded in John 3. You must be born again, he said, not of water like a natural birth, but of spirit. Unlike the first one, the second birth is everlasting. It will never see death. In Genesis' creation story God blew life into Adam. Jesus now blew a new life into his followers. This 'holy spirit' issues from the Holy Spirit, the third Person of the Trinity.

Jesus appeared walking in through a wall. He seemed very much a human person, whose wounds from the cross Thomas could touch. He was human, but of a different kind and would have looked radiant. Jesus was the first person, first in all of the natural world, who came to embody the renewed creation God started after the total defeat of sin. It all was very strange to his disciples. Days later, when alone with their confusion, they went fishing.

13

A New Creation

What happened early morning of that first Easter is told somewhat differently in each of the four Gospels. After all, they were written much later mostly from hearsay and memory. Apostle John recounts how when some of the disciples having heard of Jesus' body disappearing found the tomb empty and left, Mary Magdalene lingered. She looked into the tomb and saw two angels asking her why she was weeping. 'Because they have taken my Lord away and I don't know where to.' Then someone behind her, whom she assumed to be a gardener, asked her the same question. When the man mentioned her by name, to her astonishment, she recognised Jesus. He told her not to touch him for he was yet to present himself to his Father.

It was a grieving woman who first met the risen Christ. Graciously the Lord must have planned it so. That the renewed Jesus appeared on earth before doing so in Heaven confirms how much his death and resurrection is a human story. As Son of God, the Lord fully identifies with humanity. He asked Mary to tell his followers that, 'I am ascending to my Father and your Father, to my God and your God.' God and people are united in Christ.

A divine perspective of Jesus' resurrection involves the primary nature of creation. He once commented that no one would take his life from him. He had the God-given power to lay it down and take it up again (John 10:18). He did exactly that at the cross and at his resurrection. In his rising Jesus became a renewed human being and concurrently a different Son of God. No longer the Son in whom the creation was doomed to suffer due to sin. The Son had disempowered sin and in him a new creation became possible. One that exists solely in divine love.

Though happening on earth, Jesus' suffering, his victory over sin, and his resurrection, translated into the Trinity as an event beyond space and time. It reverberated throughout the material and spiritual world, forwards and backwards. What we call past and future, both holding together in the Son, it had become redeemed through the rising of Jesus of Nazareth.

From an earthly perspective redemption, within the space and time of universal love, will gradually work itself out. It began once Jesus rose to meet his Father as a renewed person. Once again God created, but now of a kind upon which sin has no hold. In the Genesis story Adam and Eve are the last to be created. This time the process is reversed. People are the first to be invited into the new. Apostle Paul formalised this insight in his teaching and boldly declared that believers in Christ are a new creation. Sin is still operative and will be until the moment God declares all to become renewed, including nature. A deed that will banish sin by divine command from our present creation. Nobody knows when this will be.

Heaven awaits and, not belonging to our temporal realm, it already exists in the Son's redeeming love for all to enter after death. Without the Son's victory there would not be a heaven. And that victory is total; with sin unable to hold onto any aspect of creation and steal it away from God's love permanently. 'It is finished,' Jesus said.

14

I AM

When Moses was instructed by God to lead Israel out of its oppression in Egypt, he asked who he would tell the people had sent him. What was God's name? Tell them I AM has sent you, came the response. It is not what we would call a name, like the word God is not a name. I AM is more like a category of being. With God that involves Ultimate Being. When once Elijah was deeply depressed, God suggested he'd stop being so negative. 'Be still and know that I AM.'

The Good News story of the Father, Son and Holy Spirit, belongs to the level of I AM. This realisation is central to approaching God's Gospel correctly. It must be treated with the respect it deserves and accepted as it has been revealed. All human knowledge is open to question, including that about the idea of God, but not the Gospel. Those insights are sacred.

It is quite a statement to make. However, we are referring

to what being alive *really* is about and that should rate highest. In our world truth is hard to find, but somewhere there must be just that and with a capital T. Not a truth so qualified by our preferences and susceptibility to misinformation, but a beacon of light that rises well above the fray. The Gospel is that beacon, a divine wisdom of love that is not human, but directed towards the plight of humanity all the same.

The history of God and people is a confusing one. The Bible records how the workings of God have been perceived over many centuries, from moments of high praise and insight to those less admirable. Opinions have differed, often considerably, with the idea of God being adapted to what is deemed expedient. The often negative treatment of prophets, with Jesus not excluded, confirms it. Religion always has a varied history. In our Christian era it is no different.

In a world where everyone will become hurt, and potentially so in church, what may be safely held onto with regard to belief? It is the Gospel; not as a mere spiritual understanding, but as an engagement with God's Love. A firm belief in the truth and active love of God's Good News is the best anchor in life one could wish for. Whatever the happenings, whatever the ideas bandied about on all and everything, including religion, whether interesting or indifferent, the Good News will be the rock in any sea of change.

In presenting God's divine story, I have selected a certain knowledge while allowing for personal interpretation. How accurate might that be? Well, the story is based on information gathered from Scripture and reputable sources, while adhering to a revealed divine perspective. Though engaging with humanity, the Gospel is not a human story. Even so, the telling needs to make sense and be readily understood by anyone so inclined. Whereby mystery must be accepted as truth where needed. The Gospel belongs to I AM.

15

A New Spirit

Thank you for reading this far. If you found it interesting and it resonates please continue. God's Good News, though a divine wisdom, is relevant to everyday living. The basis of this relevancy is not merely information but transformation. Jesus foretold this with the comment that a believer would be born again in spirit. An act by God that should be wisely guarded. Jesus was strong on that point. His comment that unless you leave father and mother you cannot be his disciple has confused many. It is not referring to literally leaving, but to not allowing cultural norms and traditions to modify his teaching – dilute its potential. For the new spiritual birth to bear fruit something uniquely personal is required. The guidance found in a relationship with the Lord.

I know my sheep and they know me, said the Lord. I am the Good Shepherd who, unlike many false ones, will safely lead them. I am the door into abundant living. For such living to become real a focused attention is needed. That focus is the Lord himself. It is not a religious focus but a personal one – one person engaging with another Person.

It is in no sense a restrictive relationship as is so often believed. Quite the opposite. The Lord asks for nothing that isn't part of careful and caring living. Wellbeing and creativity become enthused. The soul is healing and the spirit strengthens. My view is that being a Christian is a privilege. A way of life offered by the Lord that needs my wholehearted attention. His presence never fails.

Being born anew of 'holy spirit' is a matter of heart and spiritual vision – of a captivation with the Lord. He will engender and nurture this worship within anyone so inclined. Though mysterious it feels very natural. Much of Christian life is seemingly mundane while yet the Lord is active. A genuine and humble call towards him will be immediately heard and responded to. Jesus is never hard to find. Be aware of his presence and the new spirit within will flourish. God's grace enables believers in special ways.

It is not religious statements and declarations of God's intent in human affairs that make the Gospel relevant in our world. Rather, it is the Gospel working its 'magic' in people individually. Within those who believe it worth their full commitment and who seek to live in accordance with the nature of Christ. They may attend church or not. What matters is the right disposition of soul and God will know.

God has set a new creation in motion, which people are invited into. The new is unlike the old, but the principle of love upholding both never changes. Those attracted by what Christianity really should be about will aspire to be people of love. Not just love as a feeling, but love in action through kindness and care. Jesus treasures the freedom of love in people and discourages any idea that would place love under rules and regulations. Such as separating Catholic and Protestant graves within areas of a cemetery. Love knows not kind or kin.

Not prioritising love and mercy shows the Gospel not being that well understood. Call it the 'shalom' test. Aspiring to shalom will be a struggle at times but the task is doable with the help of a Lord who understands. When I fail, I don't worry about it, and try again. I will never be perfect, nor seek to be. Mistakes, properly reflected on, foster humility, which is a good thing.

16

Come

What might a relationship with Jesus be like? Not limited to rites and rituals, that is for sure. An engagement with the Lord is of an altogether different nature. Its insights originate from God directly. It is a matter of heart, with the Lord knowing those willing to follow his ways. The Lord is kind and the sternness that sometimes portrays God is nothing like him.

Jesus says, 'Come to me, all who labour and are heavy laden and I will give you rest. Take my yoke upon you, and learn from me; for I am gentle and lowly in heart, and you will find rest for your souls. For my yoke is easy, and my burden is light' (Mat. 11:28-30).

This was spoken to folk burdened under the demands of Jewish authority and tradition. But it is just as pertinent today when facing the pressures of modern society with its expectations for me to *be* someone. No time for losers for we are the champions, Queen proudly sings. Human perspectives on what counts most can be egocentric and potentially cruel. Quite unlike Jesus.

The Good News opens up to a different realm of living altogether, a higher realm. 'Come to me,' the Lord says. Not so that I can insist on how life is to be lived, but for me to help you in making the best of it. Find the true way in which to be human and it will bring rest to your soul. I will be kind and gentle in my suggestions, with ideas you are well able to execute.

Jesus warmly invites to learn from him. In life, things worthwhile are achieved by seeing opportunity and a firm commitment to its possibilities. Capability rates highly, so it is thought. Not so with the Lord, who considers talent less important than desire. Whether I am willing to learn and put the yards in is what matters.

With regard to spirit, much has been written about what such learning is like. I'm fairly well read-up on it including doing spiritual exercises. It has been helpful and needed information, but not pivotal. My sensitivity towards the Lord has been from the beginning of being a Christian while knowing little. Always, I have talked with him in my spirit. Through the years, I have learned most about being a genuine Christian from managing life and its challenges the Good News way. Like seeking to live out the fruits of the spirit such as patience, kindness, faithfulness and self-control (Gal. 5:22-23).

The important skills in matters of spirit and soul are learned on the way. I don't need a 'learners permit' with instructions prior to traveling. The ways of the Lord are inherent to personhood and never dormant within those who truly love him. Ways, in which the knowledge of good and evil features prominently. Everyone is able to commit to that. Do so with Jesus and other aspects of the fruit of the spirit become realised also. Those of feeling God's love and joy and peace.

17

Religion

The history of religion through the ages is so diverse and multifaceted that a brief comment like mine will never do it justice. Religion is a social contract including rituals, teachings and holy places that instils and maintains belief in a greater realm of spirits. It is guided by authority and becomes a tradition. Religion addresses spiritual realities and seeks to appease those. The gods are multiple or just the One.

Christianity finds it origin in the Jewish faith. It was to the Israelites that the One God began to reveal the divine presence. God understands the need for religion as it facilitates worship and consistency of belief within a society. Moses was instructed to build a Tabernacle and set up a Priesthood. Not that God thereby became well understood or followed. At one point God lamented that because people were prospering under divine blessings, they had forgotten and ignored the origin of those.

The problem with religion is, as with everything else significant in human affairs, that it involves people. And people are subject to the influences of sin. Inevitably religion is exposed to those dynamics. History is full of religious misdemeanours and cruelty. With Christianity that happens while simultaneously representing a God who is love. Surely, much good is done in the name of the Lord, but much fails the 'shalom' test.

Christianity has a rich tradition of wisdom, art and festivals. Beautiful music to be enjoyed and fine projects of mercy to join. Significant meaning is to be found in worship that facilitate a spiritual engagement with the Lord. I will never encourage someone to leave church but I understand when believers do. I have seen people being badly hurt in Christian affairs and others becoming disillusioned. The spiritual nourishment once found had disappeared.

God is relational and not religious. Religion can assist in finding God, but cannot make it happen. It is the Lord himself who says, 'Come'. A believer's response may be within a religious context though that isn't a must. God's Good News needs not religion and exists above it. It will never discourage religious engagement, but it is relevant regardless of the situation a person might be in.

I have no idea what your situation is like, but God is near. Perhaps you once asked the Lord for the forgiveness of sins, which is a good thing. Perhaps you go to church and perhaps you don't. You may be well versed in the Bible or little. If the latter, why not find some readings on God's love, on prayerful reflection and contemplation. When familiar with spiritual exercises please continue. Above all, live in a way that corresponds with what Jesus is like, as best you can. God will be pleased.

Put your trust in the Lord and let not doubt waylay you. Doubts always arise and must be countered by faith and confidence. The Lord is closer than breathing, whatever life may bring. Religion, wisely administered, he appreciates. But it is people he is focused on.

18

The Preacher

In the Old Testament is a book called Ecclesiastes, or The Preacher. Its writer tries to figure out the meaning of life and cannot make sense of it. After much reflection he concludes that all is vanity and a blowing after wind. The best response to life is to love God, family and work, and enjoy the occasional party. There is little point in being wise and smart in our sorry lives. 'For in much wisdom is much vexation, and he who increases in knowledge increases sorrow' (1: 18).

It all seems negative. But the book isn't suggesting not having a go, rather that when you do, that you keep life in perspective. You are limited in true understanding and easily led astray by desires assigning excessive value to that which is transient. It also suggests that for all our cleverness, we don't really know what is going on. Are we being played by forces beyond our control?

In interpreting religious texts definitive answers remain

elusive. Deliberations and theological insights have their value, but it is limited. Disputes in understanding God never end. I enjoy trying to figure out what it means *to be* and have done so for years. Some of it has been helpful. In the end though I came to the conclusion that the one knowledge about God that would stand the test of time is the Gospel. And mostly that is a matter of faith rather than reason.

I have come to accept that much of life I have no answer to, at least not one that makes a difference in changing things. Suffering is a good example. Its origin is found in the power of sin. Sin is still operative and thus creation suffers. God never afflicts suffering. Not even on Jesus who, on the cross, took the excruciating experience of sin's full power freely upon himself.

    I know of a mother whose son died young of cancer. She was wondering whether it was a punishment for her having done wrong, which she hadn't. God forbid! There is so much suffering about and always it is because of natural causes or because of what humanity brings upon itself. Yes, the Lord does miracles at times to alleviate problems. I am familiar with those. God answers prayers positively many a time in other matters. Generally though suffering is with us to stay.

So, what would be my best response? Brother Lawrence (c.1614-91), who is known for his profound experiences of the presence of God, simply decided that whatever came upon him, God knew about it and would help him see it through. Lady Julian found the Lord telling her that he would be with her in her sufferings, as he would be with anyone. All nice, but not much of a solution you might say. Seems that way. But the Lord's presence *does* make a difference, when I am in trouble.

19

With the flow

It is a challenge being a person. We are thrown into life at the deep end and learn as we go. The river of life is full of surprises. It bends, has the occasional rapids and a few still waters. In it all I am busy keeping my head above water. Though there are many others around me going with the flow of the river their own way, deep down, I feel out of my depth. Deep down in my soul I feel alone. Nobody truly understands me and I often don't myself. Life is a rugged affair that throws all kinds at me. The river is sort of murky and definitely seems impersonal. Woe, is me!

God's Good News is the story of cleaning up that river and smoothing out its currents. But the story itself is of little use in managing the flow. For that I need the Lord, a helper in life. The river may be impersonal but the Lord never is. The river leads into unforeseen and sometimes difficult places, but the Lord of the river has the floaty handy. I may not know where I am going, but he does. Life within my soul is a lonely business. Only I can live it out and in my way. But the Lord brings another reality into it – his presence. I am no longer alone.

The Lord knows me better than I will ever do myself. Sure, I have abilities and particularities. Some things I am good at and others not so. In given areas, other people are far more capable than I. The Lord has no interest in changing that. I am welcome to be what I am like. It is the rough edges that need smoothing out and that for my own benefit. It is the learning I will have to do to find calm waters. The Lord knows and is patient.

Everyone has the choice whether to go down the river singularly or accept company within their spirit. The Good News ensures that such company may be easily found. The Person in whom all exists and who has gained total control over creation, is on standby to call on. A Person, who is love personified.

The Gospel reveals divine realities and in doing so offers a frame of reference as to what life really is about. No longer do I have to wonder regarding the meaning of it all. Surely, it requires faith, which isn't unreasonable. The Gospel offers important answers, but not to everything.

A relationship with Jesus brings additional understanding. Insights that concern personhood and spirituality. How to live a relational life well and come before the Lord in rest and confidence.

None of this is immediate and all of it my choice. I need patience and have to overcome discouragement: two qualities the Lord particularly values. In the end though it all depends on what my heart desires. Has my vision been captivated by the Lord and the possibilities he has for me? Like the blind man who asked Lord, 'make me see'. The Lord will, if I allow him to. No longer do I have to drift alone.

20

In this world, not of it

Jesus prayed that his disciples might be steadfast in their belief. That his Father might always look after them. My followers are in the world but not of it, Jesus said. Please guard their lives. It corresponds with the Good News: it is not of this world but definitely in it. It offers truth worthy of belief, no matter what. It is active through Jesus and brings superior knowledge. Not thereby to write off other knowledge about God, but it comes in secondary; ideas open to discussion to which a definitive answer is not always possible.

As a believer I do feel somewhat as if being in two places. One firmly anchored into life on earth and another that intuitively reached for a greater realm to which I belong as well. I know it to be a realm of light without shadows, but presently see it dimly. Not so my earthly outlook in which I see everyday life well enough, full of confusion and misinformation. I have to make the best of it, try to find some wisdom and some peace.

I have long given up seeking to understand everything. For that reason I like The Preacher. Per example, I am a universalist and thus believe that all will be saved. It is a position held by many a reputable biblical scholar these days. It supports my understanding of the Gospel. Still, it poses an obvious question. So it doesn't matter then, how I behave while on earth?

Jesus made pretty sure in explaining that it does. Evil will not remain unnoticed. Such as the millstone around someone's neck who wilfully damages the wellbeing of children. Apostle Paul speaks about the judgment seat of Christ to be faced by Christians. Those who live deeply immoral lives will be saved as if through fire. And then there is hell; does it actually exist? Modern scholarship seriously doubts it. There are many examples in Scripture of unwise behaviour having consequences. In light of God's all-saving love this is confusing. In my view though it is the Gospel that matters most and that information is clear enough.

The idea of judgment should not trouble anyone who lives a decent life, nothing perfect but good enough. The Lord never seeks vengeance and ever seeks to embrace.

The divine wisdom is higher than ours and surely also with regard to wrongdoing. As Lady Julian heard Jesus so clearly say: 'What is impossible to people's understanding, is possible with God' (c.f. Mt. 19: 25-26).

The question asked about behaviour and God is fair, but it misses the important mark. The real question is, when aware of the heart of God and the Good News, whether I am willing to follow Jesus well. If so, under his guidance unwise behaviour will begin to fall in line, over time. The Lord's love is covering all my mistakes and I will be free of judgments upon me. My spirit will prosper and my soul rejoice. With serious mistakes I humbly ask the Lord for help towards betterment. Always, he is encouraging.

There are two ways of looking at the Good News: the human view that has troubles in seeing clearly and the divine view that seeks to come across. Have faith in the divine and the human will be supported by an ever present Lord in special ways. No-one is excluded from the invitation to join in. Everyone can be successful, when wholeheartedly committing. We are loved. God *is* Love.

21

Best wishes

Build your house properly on rock and it will withstand anything, Jesus advised. The Gospel is that rock and I am the house. It is a simple building for myself and a visitor – if I let him in. In life there are many foundations to choose from. The airwaves and culture are full of ideas. But my foundation is the Good News that shines forth brightly through the windows.

That light is an inward and spiritual event. Its source is the visitor, who is willing to make permanent residence. He is a kind and caring presence, never angry and brings inner strength. I'm in safe and perfect hands. Just him and me.

God and Gospel has been written in the knowledge that spiritually we are singular beings, who are indwelled by the spirit of God and invited into the reality of God's presence. The nature of the human spirit is as such that it can feed off all kinds of inputs. Life is an unfolding reality of continued choices and temptations. Ever, I keep the

Preacher in mind, who in seeking for the meaning of life found solace in a focus on God.

People are singular beings in community. Interacting with others, and nature as well, ensures our development. It is impossible to grow healthily in isolation. My house stands with other dwellings nearby. Once I shut my door though, deep down, I feel alone, but for the Lord.

The surrounding houses are important as I will learn from them. Their occupants help, disappoint or hurt me. Regularly, I will retreat to kneel on my foundation that is the Good News. Then I step out again in the knowledge that wise living requires community. That may include church. The Christian story has unfolded through church progressively for better or worse. The Christian spiritual tradition has a wealth of advice about living with God. Finding the Lord in community with others is precious. It may be problematic as well.

You may not feel to join church. You may have left church behind, like so many. Has thereby a meaningful life with Jesus invariably been lost? It need not be so. The Gospel belongs to the world and not to the church exclusively. It belongs to Jesus, who will engage with anyone seeking him out.

Reading in the New Testament enriches the relationship with the Lord. Find an easy language version and take note of the Gospel of John, which is a favourite of many. When Scripture confuses don't worry about it. Live out the Good News and you'll be fine. If possible converse with a friend about Christian living in non-judgmental ways. Encourage each other and make humility your aim.

Above all, keep talking to the Lord in mind and heart as much as possible. Discuss everything with him and your intuition will guide you. Acknowledge your deep-seated hurts and ask for healing. Have some quiet times. Make sure to read up regularly, at least for a bit, on Christian wisdom.

Travel safely with the Lord. I wish you well,

Michael

Three little books, *Walking with God*, *Being with God* and *A Feel for God*, are available from my website in a print version or as free ebooks. As is this present one. They may be of help. Please use the link *adbooks.online*.

Milton Keynes UK
Ingram Content Group UK Ltd.
UKHW021026111024
2113UKWH00026B/433